LEADING LADY

BARBARA BUSH

Written by:
Rosemary Wallner

Published by Abdo & Daughters, 6535 Cecilia Circle, Edina, Minnesota 55439.

Library bound edition distributed by Rockbottom Books, Pentagon Tower, P.O. Box 36036, Minneapolis, Minnesota 55435.

Library of Congress Number:91-073028   ISBN: 1-56239-079-1

Photos by Wide World Photos: 5, 14, 19, 20, 25, 26, 29, 31, 32
            Bettmann Newsphotos: 6, 21, 23

Edited by: Bob Italia

TABLE OF CONTENTS

THE SILVER FOX

Since January 1989, when her husband was sworn in as president of the United States, Barbara Bush has been in the nation's spotlight. Reporters have asked her about every aspect of her life including her clothes, hair, family, and lifestyle.

What does Barbara Bush think about all the attention and the honor of being First Lady? "I think the most surprising thing for me has been how much I've loved it," exclaimed Bush. "I can hardly wait to get up every morning."

Bush, whose children have given her the nickname "The Silver Fox," has lived in twenty-nine houses in seventeen cities since she married George Bush in 1945. She has seen her husband rise from an oil executive to president of the United States. She has survived the death of a child and raised four sons and a daughter. One friend described Bush as a "combination of gentleness and steel."

As First Lady she stands by her husband and family while volunteering to help others whenever possible.

First lady Barbara Bush holds the bible for her
husband George as he is being sworn in on January
20, 1989 as President of the United States.

Many people have grown to admire all she has done for her family and others. In late 1990 Bush told a reporter, "I suspect people might like me a bit because I remind them of how things ought to be and how *they* ought to be."

Barbara Bush waves the American flag in celebration of her husband's nomination for president.

GROWING UP IN RYE, NEW YORK

Barbara Pierce was born on June 8, 1925, and lived in the wealthy neighborhood of Rye, New York. She was the third of four children of Marvin and Pauline Pierce. Bush's father was a publisher for *McCalls* magazine; her mother stayed home and raised Bush and her brothers and sister.

When Bush was seven years old, her family found out that her youngest brother Scott had a cyst in the bone marrow of his shoulder. Pauline Pierce spent all her time at the hospital with Scott and little time with Bush. "My mother, I'm sure, was tired and irritable and I didn't understand it at the time," said Bush years later. "But I guess I felt neglected, that she didn't spend as much time on me… Now as a mother and grandmother, I realize what she was going through."

As a result, Bush said, "I was much closer to my father and probably the least close to my mother."

Young Barbara Pierce was popular, fun-loving, and outgoing. She idolized her older sister Martha and kept close to her father. "I was brought up with a strong sense of family loyalty," she remembered. "My father cherished every word of his four children. He really cared about us."

In 1931, six-year-old Bush entered Rye's Milton School. On the first day of classes, Bush's mother took her daughter to meet the new teachers and then left without saying good-bye. "I felt abandoned," recalled Bush. "But I truly loved school so much I forgave her by the time I got home."

Bush stayed at Milton through sixth grade and then entered a private day school. When she was a junior in high school, Bush transferred to Ashley Hall in Charleston, South Carolina.

In December 1941, the United States entered World War II. That same month, sixteen-year-old Barbara came home for the holidays and went to a dance at the Round Hill Country Club in Greenwich, Connecticut. There she met seventeen-year-old George Herbert Walker Bush. George asked her to dance and she accepted. But the band began to play a waltz. Because George didn't waltz, the two sat down and began to talk. "I could hardly breathe when he was in the room," said Bush, describing the effect George had on her.

After the Christmas holidays, Barbara went back to Ashley Hall and George went to his school in Andover, Massachusetts – a thousand miles away. The two kept in touch by writing letters. Later in 1942, George took Barbara to his senior prom.

When George turned eighteen years old in June 1942, he enlisted in the Navy. A year later, he became the Navy's youngest pilot. Before he began his advanced flight training, George invited Barbara to Walker's Point, his family's summer home in Kennebunkport, Maine.

For two weeks in the summer of 1943, Barbara, George, and George's family spent time in the Bush's fifteen-room, seven-bath country home. That summer, George and Barbara became secretly engaged. A few months later, George was assigned to a torpedo squadron in the Pacific Ocean and Barbara enrolled in Smith College in Northampton, Massachusetts. The two were uncertain about their futures, but were deter- mined to stay together despite the war.

BARBARA AND GEORGE

In 1944, Barbara dropped out of Smith College and began to plan her wedding, which was set for December. In September, however, George's plane was hit by flak during a raid on a Japanese target. As his plane went into a dive, George ordered his two crew members to bail out. George parachuted out soon after and landed in the sea.

Although he suffered from a head wound, George kept afloat long enough to be rescued by an American submarine (George's crew members died in the crash). Months later, he rejoined his squadron and was able to get word to his family that he was safe.

While George was missing in action, his parents kept the news from Barbara. She found out that he had been shot down only a few days before the family received word that he was safe. George returned home on Christmas Eve. He was twenty years old and a veteran of 58 combat missions.

On January 6, 1945 (19 days later than they had planned), Barbara and George were married at the First Presbyterian Church in Rye. "I married the first boy I ever kissed," said Barbara proudly. The couple spent the first few months of their married life moving from one military base to another. Barbara feared that George's squadron would be called up again for duty but that didn't happen.

When the war ended in August 1945, George enrolled in Yale University where he majored in economics. Barbara packed up and moved to New Haven, Connecticut, with her husband. On July 6, 1946, their first child, George Walker Bush, Jr., was born.

In June 1948, George graduated from Yale. For a time the Bushes considered buying a farm. George, however, was drawn to Texas, where the oil boom was on. He worked at a large oil company for a year before being transferred to California where he worked as a salesman selling drill bits. He often traveled 1,000 miles a week making sales calls.

In 1949, Barbara's mother and father were in a serious car accident. Barbara's mother was killed and her father was injured. Barbara was unable to go to the funeral because she was seven months pregnant with her second child. Her father persuaded her not to travel because it was such a long distance, but Barbara regrets that decision. "I'll never forgive myself for not going to my mother's funeral or spending time with my father in the hospital," she confessed. Their daughter Robin was born a few months later.

The next year, George decided to move his family back to Texas so he could start his own oil company. Once again Barbara packed up the household and children and followed her husband to a new job in Midland, Texas. A second son, John (Jeb) Bush was born in Midland. Barbara remembered the next few years fondly.

"There were very dormant years in there where I was perfectly happy to have children," she said. "I always did volunteer work, but I didn't do anything imaginative or creative. George was building businesses all around the world, and we couldn't afford for me to go to those places with him."

In early 1953, the Bushes learned that their young daughter had leukemia, a non-curable form of cancer. Although they took her to several cancer specialists in New York, three-year-old Robin Bush died in October. "I just fell apart when Robin died," Barbara Bush remembered years later. "I hadn't cried at all when she was alive, but after she died I felt I could cry forever."

To help her cope with the pain, Bush began to do volunteer work for the city of Midland. She established a thrift shop to help clothe people in the poorer sections of town. She also volunteered at Midland Memorial Hospital.

"Life has its bumps," said Bush. "We should enjoy ourselves during the good times and make the most of the bad times."

After Robin's death, the Bushes had three more children. Neil was born in 1955, Marvin in 1956, and Dorothy (Doro) in 1959. As George's business became more successful, he continued to travel. Bush was alone with her children much of the time, but she didn't mind. "It was a period for me of long days and short years [with] short chubby arms around your neck and sticky kisses," she said.

As her eldest son recalled later, the Bushes were a close family. "I've never heard my mother or father utter a harsh or ugly word to each other," George, Jr., said. "They have always had a home of love. They love each other and there was no question that they loved us."

The Bushes were a very close family — pictured here at their home in 1964.

A POLITICAL CAREER BEGINS

By the early 1960s, George Bush decided to explore areas that were not part of the oil business. His father was a United States senator and in 1964 George also decided to try for the Senate.

Although that campaign was unsuccessful, George was elected to Congress in 1966 and the whole Bush family moved to Washington, D.C. George served four years with Congress until he was named the United Nations ambassador in 1971. That meant another move for the Bushes, this time to New York City.

While in New York, Bush volunteered at the cancer center where her daughter had been treated 20 years earlier. Every Tuesday and Thursday, she helped out wherever she was needed.

Another move came in 1974 when George was named the U.S. representative to China. George and Barbara Bush, along with their cocker spaniel, arrived in Beijing, China, in October. What the Bushes didn't find out until later was that the Chinese had gotten rid of all their dogs to stop the spread of disease. When Bush took her dog for a walk, many people did not know what the animal was. Some pointed to the dog and said, "Mao!" which is the Chinese word for cat. Many Chinese people were afraid of the dog. Bush had to continually reassure people that he was only a little dog and wouldn't bite.

By December 1975, the Bushes traveled back to Washington, D.C., because President Gerald Ford had named George director of the Central Intelligence Agency (CIA). The move back to Washington was hard for Bush. In China, she had spent a lot of time with her husband, bicycling, sightseeing, and visiting friends. Now, much of George's job was top secret and it was necessary for him to spend a lot of time away from home. Bush's children were grown and for the first time she began to have doubts about her role as a wife and mother.

For six months, she suffered severe depression. "I would feel like crying a lot and I really painfully hurt," she said, describing that time. Her husband and her volunteer work supported her through this time.

Bush became a regular volunteer at the Washington Home, a health care center for the seriously ill. After six months her depression disappeared and her love of volunteering became a large part of her life.

Bush's parents had been active in volunteering for their community charities and Bush learned by their example to help others. "I don't think anybody sat you down," she explained. "We just grew up knowing that's what you did." Her enthusiasm for volunteering continues. "You get right in and you work," she said. "You see yourself feeding the hungry, nurturing the poor."

Bush strongly believes that volunteering is a useful tool that can help ease many of America's problems including homelessness and lack of education. She says that "everybody has some-thing [to give], whether you have time or money or know-how or space."

During one of her husband's campaigns, Bush took her volunteering one step further when she started Operation Soap. She asked her husband's aids and reporters to collect hotel soaps and shampoos and donate them to the homeless.

Bush's children have always seen her volun-teering efforts in action – although they haven't always been happy about them. "I remember being jealous when my mom would run off to the Washington Home," said Marvin Bush. "It wasn't until I was older that I appreciated what she told me, that to live a complete life, you need to help other people."

As Bush volunteered her services, her husband continued his political career. In 1980, Ronald Reagan chose George as his running mate for that year's presidential election. When Reagan won the election, George became the vice president. Four years later, Reagan won the 1984 election and George continued his job as vice president. In the late 1980s, George decided to run for president and was elected in November 1988.

THE FIRST LADY

On January 20, 1989, George Bush was inaugurated as the forty-first president of the United States. All five of the Bush's children and their 10 grandchildren attended the event.

18

Barbara Bush has always volunteered her efforts. Here she helps her husband campaign for the presidency.

Bush was ready to take on the role of First Lady. She knew much about Washington's social and political scenes through her years as the wife of the vice president.

A typical day at the White House for Bush begins at 6 a.m. when she walks Millie, the Bush's springer spaniel. After breakfast with the president, her official time is spent answering mail and making personal appearances (in 1989, she visited 28 cities and 13 foreign countries).

President Bush's family gathers around him as they celebrate the inauguration.

First lady Barbara Bush watches over the family dog, Millie, and her six newborn pups.

She plans state dinners and family lunches and tries to leave room in her daily schedule for a swim in the White House's heated outdoor pool.

Being the wife of the president, Barbara Bush finds that many people want to know her views on everything from child care to gun control. But she tries to keep her opinions to herself. "I do not speak out on issues because I am not the elected official," she explained. Being quiet about certain issues is hard for an independent woman like Bush. If she thinks something is wrong, she tells George privately.

"It's not that he doesn't discuss things with me or that I might suggest such and such is great," she said, "but I don't agree with George on everything, nor does he agree with me on everything."

By the end of 1990, opinion polls said that Barbara Bush was the most admired woman in the United States. Her first two years as First Lady had been momentous. Shortly after she became First Lady, she named Anna Perez as her press secretary. Perez was the first African American spokesperson for a First Lady. As press secretary, Perez has the most visible position on Barbara Bush's staff.

Throughout her time as First Lady, however, Bush has never forgotten her love of volunteering. Her first official visit after the inauguration was to Martha's Table, a self-help center in Washington that distributes free meals to deprived children and homeless men and women. "Our success as a society depends not on what happens in the White House but inside your house," she told reporters.

Volunteering her time is very important to Mrs. Bush. Here she councils at a child abuse prevention center.

When she became the First Lady, however, she had less and less time to volunteer. "I gave hours of time. And, of course, money," she said. "Now what I can do best is highlight these programs." One organization she has continued to donate time and money to is the literacy program in the United States.

FIGHTING FOR LITERACY

"[I'll] spend fifty percent of my time on volunteer projects, charitable causes, and, of course, my fight for literacy," said Bush in a 1990 interview. Her support for literacy began in 1979 when her husband first ran for office. Bush realized that if he won, she would have a great opportunity to advance a special cause of her own.

"I once spent the summer thinking of all the things that bothered me – teen pregnancy, drugs, everything – and I realized everything would be better if more people could read and write," Bush explained. In the late 1970s, illiteracy was still hidden in the United States. But Bush learned that 23 million adults in America couldn't read or write beyond the fourth-grade level. From then on, she worked with programs that encouraged people to learn. By 1989, Bush had visited more than 500 literacy programs in libraries, schools, day-care centers, and housing projects.

In March 1989 at a White House luncheon, Bush announced the start of the Barbara Bush Foundation for Family Literacy. The foundation supports projects that teach reading skills to parents at the same time their children learn to read. Since its beginnings, the group has given $500,000 in grants to reading programs across the country.

By 1989 Barbara Bush visited over 500 literacy programs and schools. Here she holds Dominic Bines, 3, during a visit to the model learning center in Washington D.C.

But Bush did not stop there. She became an active member of Reading Is Fundamental (RIF), a group that distributes free books. She also started a radio program titled "Mrs. Bush's Story Time." During the program, which began in September 1990, Bush reads aloud favorite children's book selections.

Barbara Bush, in her efforts to call attention to the illiteracy problem, visits a reading center in East Harlem, New York.

Bush summed up her reasons for fighting illiteracy in a 1989 interview: "I believe if we can lick the problem of people being functionally illiterate – unable to read or write at the fifth-grade level – we will then go on to solve most of the other major problems besetting this country."

DISAGREEMENTS WITH WELLESLEY COLLEGE

Barbara Bush has devoted her life to her husband and children and to helping others. She has never had a career or had to work for a living. Although she grew up in an era where that was acceptable, some have disagreed with her choice. The idea of women working outside the home instead of raising a family full time became a major issue for Bush in the Spring of 1990.

Each year colleges look for someone to speak at their annual commencement ceremonies. Before graduates receive their diplomas, they listen to someone who will inspire them to do great things in their lives. The students at Wellesley College, an all-female school in Wellesley, Massachusetts, chose Barbara Bush for their 1990 speaker.

But shortly after she was chosen, 150 students signed a petition protesting the choice. The students said that Bush's success stemmed from her husband's accomplishments and not her own. The students had been taught that they would be rewarded on the basis of their own talents and not on that of a spouse. The students did not think that Bush would have any good advice to offer them.

Bush heard about the problem through newspaper and television reports. But she never thought of not going. "The point they had to remember was *they* invited me," stressed Bush. "I did not ask them to let me please come. I had 250 invitations to speak last season, and I chose them."

"You have a choice," added Bush. "You can love your life or not, and I have chosen to love my life."

Bush went to the commencement ceremonies and even brought Raisa Gorbachev, the wife of Mikhail Gorbachev, the leader of the Soviet Union. In her speech, she advised the graduates to acknowledge the differences in people. She

First lady Barbara Bush grasps Soviet first lady Raisa Gorbachevs hand in response to the Wellesley College Welcoming Statements.

stressed that not everyone will make the same choices in life. The important thing was to be happy and to do what you want to do.

"At the end of your life," she told the crowd of women, "you will never regret not having passed one more test, [not] winning one more verdict, or not closing one more deal. You will regret time not spent with a husband, a child, a friend, or a parent." At the end of her speech, the crowd wildly applauded. Bush had stood by what she believed in and had, once again, earned the praise of others.

KEEPING THINGS IN PERSPECTIVE

Through volunteering and spending time with her family, Bush has been able to meet many hardships. One recent ordeal was the discovery that she suffered from Graves Disease, a thyroid condition that affects the eyes. Although it is not life threatening, the disease is frustrating for Bush. She must put up with double vision, swollen eyes, endless doctor visits, and treatments.

Since March 1990, the disease has been treated with a series of radiation treatments. Although the effects of the disease sometimes make her irritable, Bush is able to endure the pain.

In the meantime, Bush continues to fill her days with volunteering and visiting. Through it all, her family remains the center of her concern. Even now that her children are grown, Bush encourages visits. "No matter how busy you are, we see to it that everyone is always welcome," she insisted. "You have to love your children unselfishly. That's hard. But it's the only way."

Barbara Bush's family has always been the center of her concerns. Here she is shown with her whole family on January 21, 1989 in the White House.

Bush feels good about her life but knows her time as First Lady will not last forever. "The simple fact is, George is now in power," she told one reporter. "And when the time comes that he's out, we'll both be out…George and I expect that, and we don't disdain it. We've been around too long. That's part of political life, and I'm prepared for it."

When asked when the best time of her life was, Bush is quick to answer. "Oh, that's easy," she said. "It's now, right now. But then, I would have said the exact same thing last year, and the year before, and almost every year before that."

Barbara Bush and her grand daughter, Marshall Lloyd Bush, visit with the first family's dog Millie and her six puppies.